EX LIBRIS

Muriel Hague
Hertford artist and art-lover
1925-2015

RUSKIN SPEAR

OVERLEAF
1 *Poet Laureate Afloat* (c. 1974)
Oil on board
42 x 24 in (107 x 66 cm)
Exhibited Royal Academy Summer Exhibition, 1975; Royal Academy
Retrospective Exhibition, 1980
Collection: Tony Stratton Smith

ENDPAPERS
This powerful 'abstract expressionist' painting is in fact an area of brushwork extracted from the hair of the woman in *Strawberry Mousse* (**11**). It illustrates the importance of brushwork, impasto and *matière*.

The eye moves from the gentle rippling of the water around the boat, where the poet sits motionless, contemplative, out of time, through the deep green area of the river to the swans, the freely suggested river bank, and the slim line of the sky. But always, in 'reading' this painting, the wandering eye is firmly directed back to the subject. Consider the angle of the tilted boater with the opposing angle of the line of the water as it changes from light to dark. This is the compositional device which locks the eye on to the poet's face.

The Royal Academy   Painters and Sculptors
General editor: Mervyn Levy

RUSKIN SPEAR

Mervyn Levy

Dear Muriel,
Sorry I missed you
The other day — but alls well
that ends well — .
        Best wishes
        Ruskin Spear 1986.

Weidenfeld and Nicolson
London

For Sally

Text copyright © 1985 Mervyn Levy
Paintings copyright © 1985 Ruskin Spear, unless otherwise
stated
First published in Great Britain in 1985 by
George Weidenfeld and Nicolson Ltd,
91 Clapham High Street,
London SW4 7TA

ISBN 0 297 78731 4

Designed by Joyce Chester
Typeset by Deltatype, Birkenhead, Merseyside
Colour separations by Newsele Litho Ltd
Printed in Italy

Contents

List of Plates

2 *At the Circus* (c. 1960)
Oil on canvas
30 x 25 in (76 x 63 cm)
Private collection

Biography

with Autobiographical Asides

1911 Born 30 June at 16, Overstone Road, Hammersmith, London.

1914–18 *'Survived War. My father collected pieces of shrapnel and for many years I was unable to take any interest in contemporary sculpture.'* Educated at Brook Green School, Hammersmith, for crippled children. (An attack of poliomyelitis as a child had badly affected one leg.) *'The classes were small, and the tuition excellent. There was a lot of emphasis on music – piano and violin – painting, chess, lettering and boot-making. I made at least one boot. . .'*

1926 Scholarship to Hammersmith School of Art.

1930 Scholarship to Royal College of Art.

1934 Diploma of Associateship, Royal College of Art.

1935 First teaching job: Croydon School of Art. *'The Principal was very interested in palmistry. He read my hand, decided I was promising, and offered me four days a week. My fee was 16/- for 2½ hours, plus travelling expenses.'*

1939–45 Excempt from war service because of the after-effects of polio. *'During the war I sold* Peace News *around Hammersmith Broadway, and persistently refused to see Army Doctors. . .'* Since his youth an accomplished jazz pianist, during the war years Spear played with several small bands at various clubs, bars and dance-halls, including the Mayfair Hotel.

1941–5 Taught at Sidcup, St Martin's, The Central and Hammersmith schools of art.

1942–4 Drawings for *Vogue* Magazine.

1944 Elected Associate Member of The Royal Academy.

1948–75. Tutor, Royal College of Art, London. Colleagues: Carel Weight, Rodrigo Moynihan, Robert Buhler, Rodney Burn, John Minton, Leonard Rosoman, Bateson Mason, Roger de Grey.

1949 Elected President, London Group.

1951 One-man exhibition, Leicester Galleries, London.

1953 Accompanied exhibition of British children's art to Prague, under the auspices of the British Czech Friendship League.

1954 Elected full Academician.

1955 Travelled to Czechoslovakia accompanying British contribution to a permanent international exhibition of painting and sculpture commemorating the destruction of Lidice.

1957 Exhibited Pushkin Museum, Moscow: 'Looking at People'.

1958 Altarpiece for R.A.F. Memorial Church, St Clement Danes, London.

1959 Designed murals for the Cricketer's Bar of the liner *Canberra*.

1979 Created C B E.

1980 Retrospective exhibition, The Royal Academy, London.

Now lives and works in Chiswick, London.

Commissioned portraits include: Lord Adrian, Sir Laurence Olivier, Sir Robin Darwin, Lord Ramsey, Harold Wilson, Sir Hugh Carleton-Greene, Lord Butler, Arnold Goodman, The Dowager Duchess of Devonshire, The Duke of Westminster, Sir Ralph Richardson.

Represented in many British and overseas galleries and collections, including: Aberdeen Art Gallery; The Arts Council of Great Britain, London; Beaverbrook Art Gallery, Fredericton, New Brunswick, Canada; The British Council, London; Glynn Vivian Art Gallery, Swansea; Harris Museum and Art Gallery, Preston; The Imperial War Museum, London; Leeds City Art Galleries; Magdalen College, Cambridge; The National Portrait Gallery, London; The National Theatre, London; Plymouth City Museum and Art Gallery; The Royal Academy of Arts, London; The Royal College of Art, London; The Royal Shakespeare Theatre, Stratford; The Tate Gallery, London; Trinity College, Cambridge; Usher Gallery, Lincoln.

Bibliography

Ruskin Spear RA, A Retrospective Exhibition, Introduction by Robert Buhler RA (The Royal Academy of Arts, 1980)

Television

Different Worlds: Hammersmith Through the Eyes of Two Painters – Carel Weight and Ruskin Spear. Monitor, 28 September 1958. Producer Sir Huw Wheldon. (BBC Television Archives).

Radio

Ruskin Spear in conversation with Mervyn Levy. Autobiographical: Recorded at Chiswick, 2 February 1984. Producer Sally Lunn (BBC Sound Archives).

Ruskin Spear in conversation with Mervyn Levy. Working Methods: Recorded at Chiswick, 21 March 1984. Producer Sally Lunn (BBC Sound Archives).

Ruskin Spear

English painters have a distinct flair for descriptive art. They are by nature and instinct narrative painters, ranging from the satire and humour of Hogarth and Gillray to the frankly eccentric vision of L. S. Lowry. The basic ingredients in this stream of native genius are simple: people and places in a related scenario. Historically, the idiom stems from the strong literary bias of English culture, and is natural to a virtuosity which until the second half of the eighteenth century expressed itself almost exclusively in the written word. When the visual arts eventually emerged in strength, the patterns of expression they assumed related mainly to a literary, narrative tradition. Apart from portraiture, the emphasis was very much upon people and social behaviour. In his study *Graphic Art of the Eighteenth Century*[1], Jean Adhemar writes of Hogarth — one of the seminal figures in the transition from the written word to the visual image — 'the first thing that strikes us about Hogarth's work is not its aesthetic quality, but its literary and moralizing aspect . . .' In short, it tells a story. *The Row About the Hotel Bedroom* (**3**) by Ruskin Spear provides a clear illustration of this continuing tradition. The artist is a master story-teller, often using simple — deceptively simple — images, underpinned with wit and irony. They have an edge which cuts to the bone. The painting is a brilliantly graphic comment on a common enough aspect of the battle of the sexes, but its undertones describe the complex pattern of a particular human relationship. The situation is ridiculous and trivial — but deadly: in fact a row about nothing, which is in itself an additional comment on the insufferability of human relationships. The subject is so skilfully attacked that one can hear the remarks tossed to and fro between the irate woman thumping petulantly out of the sea — her empty face livid with abuse (the painter has given her no features) — and the protesting man.

English narrative art of the eighteenth century is close to the genre of Dutch seventeenth-century painters, with their shrewd commentaries on working and domestic life, approving or critical. English and Dutch social and moral comment ran parallel. In general the subjects were also complementary. The pursuits of ordinary people — sport, music, travel and relaxation —

3 *The Row About the Hotel
Bedroom* (1984)
Oil on board
28 x 36 in (71 x 91 cm)
Private collection

were all closely documented. Dutch genre
painting and eighteenth-century English
graphic art were much concerned with
taverns and drinking, themes which already
provide a direct link with the Hammersmith
pubs of Ruskin Spear (**36**). The most striking
and apt comparison would be between the
artist's bar scenes and the taverns of Adriaen

Brouwer (1606–38).

Ruskin Spear was born in Hammersmith in 1911, the son of a coach-painter. He was given the remarkable christian names of Augustus John Ruskin. They were chosen by his mother, not because she had any awareness of the prophetic significance of her choice, but quite simply because the infant's father was Augustus and her father John. She was at the time of the birth in service as a cook with a family interested in the arts, and they had a son named Ruskin. Hence the third name. In the event the choice was more than apt.

At the age of fifteen Ruskin Spear won a scholarship to the Hammersmith School of Art, and in 1931 a scholarship to the Royal College of Art. Here, under the tutelege of

4 *Old Man on a Couch*
(c. 1932)
Black and white chalk
10 x 12 in (25 x 31 cm)
Exhibited Royal Academy
Retrospective Exhibition,
1980
Collection: Lady
Gwendolen Herbert

The subject is the artist's
father.

5 *Study in the Victoria and
Albert Museum* (1934)
Pencil
12 x 7 in (31 x 18 cm)
Collection: the artist

A drawing made while the
artist was a student at the
Royal College of Art. The
intense concentration of
the artist and the frailty of
old age are conveyed with
great economy. One can
feel the gripping dedication
of the hands and the
tiredness of the legs.

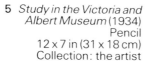

13

Sir William Rothenstein, with his insistence that the craft of drawing was the most fundamental of first principles, the young painter, by nature a fine draughtsman, laid the foundations of his art. Drawing was the key, as much for him as for Rembrandt or Jackson Pollock. But it was Sickert and the Camden Town Group who exerted the most profound influence upon him during those early, formative years. As his close friend, the painter Robert Buhler, remarks in his introduction to the catalogue of the artist's retrospective exhibition at The Royal Academy of Arts in 1980: 'One could say that Ruskin Spear has done for Hammersmith what Sickert did for Camden Town. Sickert, although of Danish origin, was by temperament well suited to work in the English

6 *Seduction* (1982)
Oil on board
36 x 28 in (91 x 71 cm)
Private collection

7 *A Night out for Muriel*
(1984)
Oil on board
40 x 30 in (101 x 76 cm)
Exhibited Royal Academy
Summer Exhibition, 1984
Private collection

8 *In the Club* (*c.* 1960)
Oil on canvas
30 x 25 in (76 x 63 cm)
Private collection

A free, loosely painted,
evolving impression which
illustrates my view that
painting is 'a moving
target'.

tradition. He started off as an actor but, as a painter, was soon attracted by the music-hall with its affectionate irony and its bawdy and colourful spectacle. Sickert's painting of this period must have appealed to Ruskin Spear's temperament. From Hogarth onwards there has always been a strong element of satire, moralizing, parabolizing and story-telling in English painting.'

And it is this stream, this thread of narrative satire with which, through Sickert, Ruskin Spear is most closely allied and in sympathy.

There are, however, two distinct branches of the idiom. One follows the path of personal eccentricity, in itself a notable feature of English art from Blake onwards. Other painters who took this route include such artists as Stanley Spencer and L. S. Lowry. Their interpretation of the narrative scene is filtered through a vision related to personal idiosyncrasies and quirks. An example is Lowry's stubborn refusal to leave the bowler hats, big boots, shawls and ill-

9 *Man Selling Postcards*
(1946)
Oil on board
30 x 26 in (76 x 66 cm)
Exhibited Royal Academy
Retrospective Exhibition,
1980
Collection: The Hon
Edwina Sandys

fitting clothes of the 1920s, irrespective of whether he was painting then or in 1970, because, as he told the author, he was 'happiest' in that period. The poverty and working-class shabbiness of the Twenties was the background of his life, and he loved it. And consider Stanley Spencer's passion for the organization of clumsy, clumping, balloonish shapes in majestic and fantastic patterns. People float – levitated – trying to separate fighting swans. Cows in a field at Cookham assume the decorative grandeur of a Gobelins tapestry. Art, certainly; but a descriptive vision which exists solely for the artist, and in his imagination.

By comparison, Ruskin Spear approaches the story he wishes to tell by the second route. He neither creates types, nor uses fantasy. With wit and affection, he lampoons the facts. This is the crucial difference between the two branches of narrative expression. Lowry and Spencer create prototypes. Spear, like Gillray or Rowlandson, exaggerates what is there. In this sense

10 *Haute Couture* (1954)
Oil on board
84 x 48 in (213 x 122 cm)
Exhibited Royal Academy
Summer Exhibition, 1955;
Royal Academy
Retrospective Exhibition,
1955; 'Looking at People',
Pushkin Museum,
Moscow, 1957
Collection: the artist

Here the concentration of
interest is upon the subject
rather than the colour,
which is delicately muted,
so that the artist's
comment is made all the
more acid.

11 *Strawberry Mousse*
(1959)
Oil on canvas
21½ x 19½ in (55 x 50 cm)
Exhibited Royal Academy
Summer Exhibition, 1959;
Royal Academy
Retrospective Exhibition,
1980
Private collection

Voluptuous greed
heightened by the vulgarity
of the woman's
accoutrements.

they are all caricaturists. The result is an
intensification of the psychological impact of
the image. Caricature is a method of psychological penetration, as many politicians
know to their chagrin. It is also a system
which relates to the distortions of Expressionist art, which is itself a form of
caricature. The grotesque, voluptuous greed
of the woman shovelling strawberry mousse
into her gaping mouth (11) is an exagger-
ation of reality, not a fiction: a statement
worthy to rank with Rowlandson, and
distinctly comparable.

During the years 1942–4 the artist made
drawings for *Vogue. In Haute Couture* (10),
which recalls that period, he uses the same
treatment, exaggerating reality to illuminate

12 *Winston Churchill*
(1956)
Oil on board
36 x 48 in (91 x 122 cm)
Exhibited Royal Academy
Summer Exhibition, 1957
Private collection

There is another version of
this subject in the
Beaverbrook Art Gallery,
Fredericton, New
Brunswick, Canada.

the horrific envy in the face of the woman on the left of the painting. In this acid statement, fashion is a demon that haunts the old and the ugly. The lust to look lovely and fashionable is crystallized in the modern fashion show, with its covens of monstrous old women. These paintings, like so many of Ruskin Spear's social commentaries, are critiques of a high order. The themes are perennial, the interpretation contemporary. People do not alter; only their disguises change. Not even the French can match us in this area of expression. They have no Hogarth, Gillray, Rowlandson or Ruskin Spear.

Closely related to these commentaries are the artist's portraits. And portraiture, by definition, is a descriptive art, for a good portrait is a description of a personality. For this reason it is also an exacting art, demanding a strength of character on the part of the painter that refuses to compromise with vanity to the detriment of the truth. Even a great portrait painter like Sargent could not endure the need to forge pleasant masks. For the last twenty years or so of his life he refused to paint portraits, preferring the far more relaxed and enjoyable pursuit of landscape painting. In the early 1900s he wrote to his friend Lady Lewis: 'I have now a bomb-proof shelter into which I retire when I sniff the coming portrait or its trajectory. . .' His refusals to undertake portrait commissions after about 1906 or 1907 are couched in the strongest terms. To one aristocratic lady enquirer he wrote: 'Ask me to paint your

13 *The Kiss* (1982)
Oil on board
48 x 24 in (122 x 61 cm)
Exhibited Royal Academy
Summer Exhibition, 1982
Private collection

gates, your fences, your barns, which I should gladly do, but NOT THE HUMAN FACE.'[2] I make this point about Sargent because, even among the greatest of portraitists, few have shown such integrity and reluctance to compromise. The small band of twentieth-century portrait painters who share these qualities include such masters of psychological penetration as Oscar Kokoschka, Otto Dix, Lucien Freud and Ruskin Spear. Every one of these painters knows that the truth lies somewhere in the blemish. Graham Sutherland, himself a great portraitist, was unfortunate in his experience with Churchill, a man of such vanity that he could accept only flattery.

Spear was luckier with his portrait of Churchill (**12**), which Lord Beaverbrook

14 *Sir Hugh Greene* (1969)
Oil on canvas
50 x 40 in (127 x 101 cm)
Commissioned by the
Governors of the BBC
Collection: BBC (copyright
© BBC)

15 *Lord George Brown*
(1981)
Oil on board
40 x 30 in (101 x 76 cm)
Exhibited Royal Academy
Summer Exhibition, 1981
Private collection

bought for his gallery in Fredericton, New Brunswick. It was painted from photographs and from numerous, searching observations of the man through television programmes. I asked the artist if Churchill had registered any reaction to the portrait when it was exhibited at the Royal Academy Summer Exhibition in 1957. 'Not really', he replied: 'He just grunted at me and the portrait and shuffled away.' The work is a piece of controlled expressionism, stressing the characteristic twist of the mouth, the sagging features and the uncertain, dangerously poised set of the spectacles. This sense

of lop-sidedness was a feature of the ageing statesman's physical aspect – a facet of decay.

Ruskin Spear's approach to the human face may not be as pathologically exploratory as that of Freud, but it is equally revealing, and certainly more witty. Spear has none of Freud's obsession with the minutiae of spots, broken veins, warts, freckles, moles, scratches, bruises or whatever else may disfigure the skin of the sitter. But he is, in a much broader sense, keenly aware of those aspects of asymmetry which are keynotes of individuality: the droop of

an eyelid, gaps in teeth, and particularly the differences between the size, shape and set of the eyes. His portraits are less disturbing than those of Freud – or Otto Dix – because however penetrating the result, the artist always seems to retain some note of humour or affection. The one approach is clinical, the other fundamentally humane.

Ruskin Spear has no hesitation in using photographs as the basis of his portraiture, either press photographs, which often provide the spark of an idea, as for *The Kiss* for instance (**13**), or private photographs of the sitter, which he usually takes himself. Sometimes he makes drawings or oil sketches from life, completing the portrait in his studio from the sketches and the photographs. Occasionally, as in the case of his

16 *Mrs Barbara Castle at the Royal Academy Banquet* (1968)
Oil on canvas
29 x 37 in (74 x 94 cm)
Exhibited Royal Academy
Summer Exhibition, 1968;
Royal Academy
Retrospective Exhibition,
1980
Private collection

17 *Harold Wilson with Pipe Smoke* (1970)
Oil on canvas
20 x 15 in (51 x 38 cm)
Exhibited Royal Academy
Summer Exhibition, 1974;
Royal Academy
Retrospective Exhibition,
1980
Collection: National Portrait
Gallery, London

portrait of Lord Ramsey as Archbishop of Canterbury (**21**), the whole picture was done from life. Anecdotes of his sitters provide rare and revealing glimpses of the nature of the relationship between the artist and his subject. Spear likes to talk to his sitters, and to encourage those typical gestures, or affectations of facial expression by which the celebrated are recognized. Sometimes, as in the case of Harold Wilson, the sitter has a carefully prepared mask which is meant to conceal his true self, but which the perceptive portraitist can read with ease. Harold Wilson, who gave Spear sittings at Downing Street, reminded him at first of Edward G. Robinson in *Little Caesar*. 'The man is a great actor,' he said, 'using his pipe as an extension of himself, stabbing with its

18 *Sir Ralph Richardson as Falstaff* (1984)
Oil on canvas
36 x 28 in (91 x 71 cm)
Commissioned by The
National Theatre, London

stem to emphasize points. We talked, mainly about tobacco as I also smoke a pipe.' Spear made a number of portraits of Wilson, drawings and paintings. The one which captures the essence of the man most completely is the smoke-wreathed portrait of him lighting up his pipe, which is now in the National Portrait Gallery (**17**). It repays analysis for it is an inventory of what the painter has seen, quite beyond the control of the sitter. The mouth sucks, the podgy hands suggest power, tenacity and control. But it is in the cunning, carefully guarded aspect of the hooded eyes that the personality of the man is laid bare. This is the exposed nerve. It is a devious face, continually watchful for the sudden thrust of an embarrassing question. The feint and the parry are already implicit in the look.

Olivier (**19**) he painted partly from life

19 *Sir Laurence Olivier as Macbeth* (1955)
Oil on canvas
$94\frac{1}{2}$ x 39 in (240 x 99 cm)
Exhibited Royal Academy
Summer Exhibition, 1956
Collection: Royal
Shakespeare Theatre
(copyright © Royal
Shakespeare Theatre)

This portrait,
commissioned by the
Governors of the Royal
Shakespeare Theatre, now
hangs in the Theatre's
picture gallery.

and partly from photographs. Talking about this commission, he told me: 'He was always late, and always charming. When he first stood in front of me with his Macbeth kit over a pin-stripe suit – glimpses of which I could see – the whole thing worried me. He looked like a whisky advert! He loved smearing his hands with red greasepaint, and even asked if he could use a tube of vermilion for the process, until I warned him

20 *Nubar Gulbenkian at
the Wellington Ball* (1965)
Oil on board
60 x 36 in (152 x 91 cm)
Exhibited Royal Academy
Summer Exhibition, 1966
Private collection

that it would be far more difficult to remove
than greasepaint! He would stand marvel-
lously for hours until, in the fading light, he
would start dropping off to sleep. I knew
then the session was over for the day.'

'Ramsey sat for me live all the way
through. Every time he entered the studio
he would raise his hands in a benign sort of
healing gesture – I suppose he was blessing
the studio, or something like that. He was an
amiable fellow, watching me continuously
from eyes hidden by those great tufted
white eyebrows. I had a devil of a job mixing
the right purple for his cassock. Purple is a
difficult colour to mix. "What are you

21 *The Rt. Rev. The Lord Ramsey of Canterbury PC*
(1964)
Oil on canvas
30 x 25 in (76 x 64 cm)
Exhibited Royal Academy
Summer Exhibition, 1965;
Royal Academy
Retrospective Exhibition,
1980
Collection: Magdalene
College, Cambridge

doing?'' he asked. ''Experimenting with purple'', I answered. And he began to echo my reply: ''Experimenting with purple . . . experimenting with purple . . .'' He went on *endlessly* repeating the phrase, each time more softly until at last it died away into silence. He hummed all the time I was painting him – hymns I suppose.'

I asked Spear about his portrait of Nubar Gulbenkian (**20**). 'Well that's a long story', he replied. 'At first Gulbenkian came to me, at one of the Academy functions, and said he would like me to paint him, and would I get in touch with his secretary and work out the details. I thought this a marvellous idea. A

lovely commission too! I envisaged painting him full length. So I rang his secretary and we had the most hideous haggle about the *size* of the picture! In the end they wanted something about a foot square! So I said no. Then a bit later on I spotted a wonderful press photograph of Gulbenkian at some ball. So I did a portrait from the photograph and put it into the Academy Summer Exhibition. It was placed right behind the President's chair, all ready for the Academy banquet. It looked good! But after the dinner, as I stood talking to Jim Callaghan, a scowling Gulbenkian stormed up to me and said: ''I never sat for you; how could you

22 *Ernie Marsh* (1954)
Oil on canvas
41 x 25 in (104 x 63 cm)
Exhibited Royal Academy
Summer Exhibition, 1955;
Royal Academy
Retrospective Exhibition,
1980
Collection: The Royal
Academy of Arts (Diploma
Work: on election to
Membership of the Royal
Academy every artist is
obliged to contribute a
'Diploma Work' to the
Academy's permanent
collection.)

Ernie Marsh is also the
central character in *Friday
Night* (**30**). Ernie often sat
for the artist, who has
expressed his fascination
for Ernie's 'wonky eyes'.

presume to paint a portrait of me?'' Then I had one of those inspired moments – they don't come often: ''Well,'' I said, ''there are lots of portraits of Jesus Christ, but so far as I know he never sat for any of them.'' It was a great moment! Jim Callaghan doubled up. Shortly afterwards I had a personal call from Nubar – all very affable, saying he wanted to be friends and inviting me to dinner. . .'

These anecdotes provide valuable clues. They disclose not only something of Ruskin Spear's working methods as a portrait painter but the range of his humour, his warmth and his keen powers of perception, both physical and psychological. But it is in the portraits of his family and his friends that his essential humanity is most apparent, although his empathy with his subject is always conveyed with restraint. This applies in particular to his portrayals of old age. The emotive content is always tightly controlled – concise and contained. It never spills over into bathos. There is compassion without sentimentality. Even in

23 *The Old Cornishman*
(*c*. 1942)
Oil on canvas
24 x 20 in (70 x 51 cm)
Collection: the artist

the study of the painter's father, drawn in 1932 (**4**) when the artist was only twenty-one, there is no excess of feeling, no self-indulgence. It is a statement about old age, brilliantly drawn and strikingly objective. I know of no better example of the artist's powers of draughtsmanship. The opposition of tension and relaxation is superbly realized in the relaxed, bowed head, the tension in the resting arm and the left leg, and the relaxation of the left arm and the right leg. The same controlled qualities illumine the study of *The Old Cornishman* (**23**). Again, the strength of the quality and realization of form is closely dependent

upon draughtsmanship. The face is in deep repose, the hands are described with a broad impressionism that suggests the continual movement of fingers clasping and unclasping as in arthritic old age, seeking positions of relief. This particular portrait makes one important and additional point. It may seem unnecessary to emphasize this, but the obvious is often overlooked, and needs to be stated. The quietude and restfulness of the conception is invested with a single note of vitality and radiance. The vertical flash of light on the old man's shirt adds just that note of brightness without which the painting as a tonal exercise would die. The point

24 *Sketch for the Portrait
of Sir Robin Darwin* (1961)
Oil on hardboard
34 x 26 in (86 x 62 cm)
Exhibited Royal Academy
Summer Exhibition, 1965
Collection: Lady Darwin

of maximum energy in a painting is the highlight. On an eyeball, or the glass in a pub, it is the switch, the point of departure into a full realization of the experience of seeing. It is magic. But it has to be placed with unerring exactitude. Hals, Manet, Ruskin Spear and countless other good painters can do this. It is not a rare facility, but it is as well to be aware of those elements of pictorial composition which are signifi-

cant. Ruskin Spear uses the switch of the highlight to maximum effect.

In general, portraits of the artist's friends, fellow Academicians and teaching colleagues from his days on the staff of the Royal College of Art lie somewhere between the polarities of satire and affection. They are keenly observed, with a sharp eye for the distinctive and characteristic features of appearance: Lowry's ill-fitting collar and

25 *Portrait of Sir Robin Darwin* (1961)
Oil on canvas
51 x 44 in (130 x 112 cm)
Exhibited Royal Academy Summer Exhibition, 1963;
Royal Academy Retrospective Exhibition, 1980
Collection: Royal College of Art

Sir Robin Darwin was Principal of the Royal College of Art from 1947 to 1971.

invariable black tie (**32**); Sir Robin Darwin's tense, authoritative stance (**25**), already crystallized in the Argus-eyed working drawing (**24**); the delightful, clown-like presence of Carel Weight – a loveable, vague dreamer, set in his own wonderland and wearing a tie purchased in Woolworth's before the Flood (**27**). All these portraits provide clues to the essential character of the subject. Occasionally, however, the essence of the man – at least as the artist understands him to be – is presented in a subtly oblique manner. What appears at first to be a compliment is in fact a critical statement. *Homage to Barnett Newman* (**26**), the American abstract painter, is based on a photograph included in a magazine article on the artist and his work. I discussed this portrait with Ruskin Spear. 'The whole thing aggravated me – and I painted it out of aggravation', he

34

told me. 'The obvious banality of second-rate abstract painting gave me the idea of standing the self-satisfied painter against one of his ludicrous canvases. I'm afraid the Homage was very much tongue in cheek! Far more to the point was the problem of painting the vast red background. Vermilion is a very expensive colour – the painting is seven feet high and four feet wide – and if it had not been for a friend who provided me with some large cans of Painters and Decorators red, the picture would have cost me a fortune! Curiously, poor old Newman died soon after I completed the painting and I was warmly complimented by one or two protagonists of the great man for my alacrity

29 *The Wave* (c. 1960)
Oil on board
40 x 50 in (102 x 127 cm)
Collection: the artist

28 *Chiswick Eyot* (1942–3)
Oil on card
18 x 36 in (46 x 91 cm)
Private collection

in producing such a speedy tribute!'

Sometimes the subject may bleed a little – a scratch here or there (12) – but Ruskin Spear is seldom a cruel portraitist. Only in the fictional characters of his satire does the claw of real savagery unsheath itself. *Haute Couture* is witness to that. Sometimes, as in the portrait of John Betjeman, *Poet Laureate Afloat* (1), he can express himself with a delicate lyricism, a quality most often to be found in his early river scenes (28). The poetic nature of his vision is in fact best expressed in his rendering of water, with its rippling undulations, its mirrors reflecting and refracting images and light. *The Wave* (29), with its spinning, rolling, spiralling convolutions of rhythmic movement is pure rhapsody.

But perhaps Ruskin Spear's most typical expressions of his warmth of feeling, his powers of observation and his deep, if detached, understanding of humanity and the environment in which he has lived and worked all his life, are to be found in his

studies of the ordinary people of West London going about their business (9), or captured in unguarded moments of relaxation. The streets and pubs and snooker halls of Hammersmith, Chiswick, Shepherd's Bush, Fulham and Putney are the areas he knows and loves. The Hampshire Hog in King Street – the setting for *Mr Hollingberry's Canary* (31), and the Ravenscourt Arms, both in Hammersmith, have always been for the artist the epitome of all that the 'local' means to its regulars. Snug and happy, gregarious or sometimes lonely (30), they provide for a while a safe world of mahogany and brass, a stage lit by the glitter and sparkle of glasses and bottles repeated to infinity in the frosted engraved mirrors. This is the Olympus of the working-man. The decor is often dull: browns, dark reds and greens; some areas lit, some in shadow. Pools of light and dark hold the habituées like fish, clutching their pints and nibbling at cigarette butts. The low tones of many of Ruskin Spear's pub pictures recall some of

30 *Friday Night* (1958)
Oil on board
47 x 39 in (119 x 99 cm)
Exhibited Royal Academy
Summer Exhibition, 1958;
Royal Academy
Retrospective Exhibition,
1980
De Beers Collection,
London

The subject is Ernie Marsh,
see Diploma Work (**22**). The
bar advertisements,
apparently placed at
random, are in fact very
cunningly positioned, and
also indicate the artist's
interest in the kind of visual
imagery that provided the
substance of Pop art.
  The deft surety of the
painter's touch in noting the
key highlights, on the
spectacles, the nose, the
glass, and the streak of
froth on the moustache, are
masterpieces of technical
virtuosity.

Sickert's paintings of the Old and the New Bedford music halls. But they are usually tuned an octave higher. Spear introduces more soaring notes of colour, both into his general palette and in his use of more brilliant overhead lighting. Certainly both painters are passionately fond of using flashes of pure red, yellow and orange, which is perhaps the one precise comparison that can be drawn. If Ruskin Spear is indebted to Sickert for stimulating his interest in locality and suggesting a tonal system for its interpretation, he redeploys these elements with an additional skill. Although he paints with a direct freshness,

Spear tightened up the much looser, broader, far less decisive style of the older master. Both are painters of dash and bravura, but Ruskin Spear contains his forms in a more tightly controlled framework. His final statements are more committed. Sickert's impressionism is amorphous, Spear's more integrated.

  Ruskin Spear paid his respects to Sickert in a painting, now destroyed, called *Ennui: 1944* (**33**). Sickert's *Ennui* was painted in about 1915, and Spear's version brings the theme of boredom up to the last year of the war, when London was still under German bombardment. The shattered house with

31 *Mr Hollingberry's Canary* (1963)
Oil on canvas
31 x 24 in (79 x 61 cm)
Exhibited Royal Academy
Summer Exhibition, 1963;
Royal Academy
Retrospective Exhibition,
1980; 1914–64 Jubilee
Exhibition of the London
Group, Tate Gallery, 1964
Collection: Harris Museum
and Art Gallery, Preston

The setting for this painting
is The Hampshire Hog, King
Street, Hammersmith.
According to the artist, the
landlord, Mr Hollingberry,
used to hang the canary
over the bar to test the
state of the air.
The subtle colour
orchestration of the
painting, based on a theme
of rich browns and lilac, is
brought to life with
highlights – the overhead
lamps, the brilliant hues of
the vase of flowers and the
yellow flash of the canary.

33 *Ennui: 1944*(1944, destroyed)
Oil on canvas
30 x 40 in (76 x 102 cm)

32 *L. S. Lowry*(1975)
Oil on canvas
40 x 30 in (102 x 76 cm)
Exhibited Royal Academy
Summer Exhibition, 1976
Private collection

collapsed walls leaves the figures of Sickert's earlier work still transfixed in the catalepsy of their timeless ennui. The idea, the artist explained, was to symbolize the tedium of the people with the apparent endlessness of the war. Beyond the two figures the gaping house opens on to streets where notices still plead for scrap to help make weapons. It is an ingenious extension of Sickert's original idea.

The artist's 'portraits' of the streets and architectural environs of West London are no less revealing than his portraits of people. Hammersmith Bridge (**35**) and the river; the Old Lyric Theatre (**51**) with its billboards; the cars, taxis, and trolley buses with their overhead wires (**34**), fix the locality with a permanence which deepens as the images recede in time and acquire the status of the timeless. The real strength of art lies in the power of the artist to invest the image with the quality of endurance. This is why abstract art *per se*, in spite of its vital role in the evolution of contemporary design, is ultimately a two-dimensional aesthetic. It is not the natural province of painting, and exists only as a cosmetic device. Lacking depth, it cannot be plumbed. The failure of

abstract art in any form but that of design or surface decoration is its inability to hold any residual potency. Only the image possesses this potential. The greater the work of art, the more it accumulates qualities of endurance. Thus Leonardo's *Virgin of the Rocks* gathers around itself intimations of the eternal. Degas dancers and women at their toilet are absolute and timeless. The aim of art is not perfection; it is endurance.

Ruskin Spear's *Hammersmith Broadway, Rush Hour, 1953* contains this power of residual endurance. It conveys a sensation of a particular time and place, a registration of fact which has found its ultimate existence out of time. It enables the spectator to move out of *his* time into the timelessness of a particular moment that has vanished from actuality but which still exists, and more potently than ever, in art. Curiously, in the process of setting out this line of thought, I discussed the Hammersmith Broadway painting with the artist, and he made the point that on looking at it again only recently it appeared to him to possess precisely that intensification of accumulated atmosphere and emotive feeling, a quality which completely transformed the remembered per-

ception of its original character. It was now a different experience. Provided the initial factual image is strongly enough felt, emotively conceptualized and, still further *re-imagined* at the time it was committed to canvas, it will inevitably acquire this fresh dimension. It will also possess the Proustian quality of time preserved through the imagination, with all the additional evocations of time regained that create an intensification of feeling and perception.

Ruskin Spear's townscapes and early family studies are those areas of his art in which this principle works most powerfully. His initial response to the factual image is so intense that endurance is a natural consequence.

This concept is well set out by Richard Morphet in his introduction to the catalogue for The Hard-Won Image, an exhibition of British art held at the Tate Gallery in 1984[3]. He writes: 'For [Francis] Bacon the art of

34 *Hammersmith Broadway, Rush Hour, 1953* (1953)
Oil on canvas
36 x 52 in (91 x 132 cm)
Exhibited Royal Academy
Summer Exhibition, 1982
Private collection

35 *Hammersmith Bridge*
(1978)
Oil on board
48 x 24 in (122 x 61 cm)
Collection: Bruce Clark

36 *In the Local* (1963)
Oil on board
29½ x 11¾ in (75 x 30 cm)
Exhibited Royal Academy
Summer Exhibition, 1963

Another view in the
Hampshire Hog (see *Mr
Hollingberry's Canary*, **31**).

Rembrandt is "much more exciting and more profound" than abstract painting because "it has been done with the added thing that it was an attempt to record a fact." In a great work "the potency of the image is created partly by the possibility of its enduring . . . Images accumulate sensation around themselves the longer they endure." ' Ruskin Spear's identification with this concept would also account for the fact that he has never been seduced by the heady chimeras of abstraction, and has always confined his art to the sufficiently exacting problem of translating the figurative image. The subject seen, noted and re-imagined is the essence of his work. But the principle only operates in those areas of

37 *Snow Scene* (1946)
Oil on board
$17\frac{1}{4} \times 23\frac{1}{4}$ in (45 x 63 cm)
Exhibited Royal
Academy Summer
Exhibition, 1947;
Royal Academy
Retrospective
Exhibition, 1980
Collection: The Tate
Gallery

expression where the intensity of vision and feeling is predominant and undistracted. In his commissioned portraits this approach is inevitably diminished by the need to establish some compromise between the requirements of the commissioning agency and the painter's resolution of the problem. This does not apply to such portraits as that of his father, or *The Old Cornishman*, any more than it would apply to the majority of Graham Sutherland's portraits, where the artist has made no compromise with the subject.

One of the chief pleasures of Ruskin Spear's art is his sense of the importance of locality – his dedicated acceptance of and delight in the area of London where he was born and has lived his life. Robert Buhler stresses this point in his Royal Academy catalogue introduction: 'Painting is a Lingua Franca which can be greatly enriched by local dialects from particular geographical areas, with their own traditional ways of looking at life. The "Art Scene" today is in danger of becoming too international, too cosmopolitan and altogether too uniform. It uses a kind of dessicated esperanto which lacks the vitality of concentrated observation of immediate local experience. . .' 'Concentrated observation of immediate local experience' is a precise and accurate description of this province of Ruskin Spear's art. He is a painter of locality as much as were Sickert and Lowry, or Raoul Dufy for that matter. But it should be emphasized again

38 *Old Woman with Roses*
(1970)
Oil on canvas
29 x 24 in (74 x 61 cm)
Exhibited Royal Academy
Retrospective Exhibition,
1980
Collection: Mrs Desmond
Heywood

See *Old Woman with Rose*
(**39**).

that, as in the case of those other artists who
have found in their own environment quite
sufficient to shape and forge a substantial
oeuvre, in Spear's work the basic elements of
his subject matter are vitalized and extended
by the process of imagination. Scenes that
he has observed in pubs or streets, cafés or
pool halls, assume a fresh dimension when
they are worked out on the easel in the
studio. The meditative evolution of these
pictures, perhaps supported by notations on
a scrap of paper or a torn up cigarette packet,
possesses an inner power which no literal,
on-the-spot documentation ever could.

A painting soon begins to assume a life of
its own, taking possession of the artist. In a
statement made to Christian Zervos in
1935[4], Picasso said: 'A picture is not thought
out and settled beforehand. While it is being
done it changes as one's thoughts change.
And when it is finished, it still goes on
changing, according to the state of mind of
whoever is looking at it. . .' So there is in all
great art this continual interplay of actuality
(which passes), imagination, and the
changes a painting imposes upon the artist
as it evolves on the canvas and, after its
completion, upon the perception of the
spectator as sensation gradually accumulates and intensifies. Painting is not a static

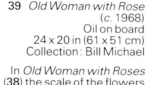

47

39 *Old Woman with Rose*
(*c.* 1968)
Oil on board
24 x 20 in (61 x 51 cm)
Collection: Bill Michael

In *Old Woman with Roses*
(**38**) the scale of the flowers
and the woman's face is
conventional, but here the
juxtaposition and relative
scale of the elements are
almost shockingly daring
and unexpected. They
seem to point to a direct
confrontation between the
face and the rose – a
parable of beauty and
ugliness perhaps?

but a dynamic and continually evolving *force majeure*.

The original experiments of Impressionist painters were necessarily static, and linked to on-the-spot observation. But once the system they wished to explore had been examined and – up to a point – proved, it was abandoned. By the mid-1880s theoretical Impressionism was exhausted. Renoir complained to his dealer Ambroise Vollard: 'About 1885 a break occured in my work. I had reached the end of Impressionism and had come to the conclusion that I neither knew how to paint nor to draw. In a word I was in a blind alley.'[5] Thereafter the Post-

Impressionists, mainly through Gauguin, Cézanne and Van Gogh, redirected the mainstream of European painting into the tributaries of Symbolism and, so far as more literal painting was concerned, along the lines of the recording of a painter's experience rather than a mere documentation of perceived natural facts. Here the emphasis was more upon structure, as in Cézanne, than upon the more diffuse qualities of Impressionism, although it would also be correct to talk of a radical revision of Impressionism in favour of statements describing contemporary experience through a modified version of the original

Impressionist technique. In England, Sickert, with his dingy Camden Town interiors and his imaginative versions of the Camden Town murder, was the prime mover towards this revised style. Ruskin Spear's only real connection with Sickert, as I have suggested earlier, is in the stimulus he received from the older master to find in 'locality' the substance of experience, to absorb its essence, and to redirect this experience through the imagination into visual sensations.

An artist needs to be studied in depth. Ruskin Spear's personality is complex and diverse. He is one of the most popular Members of the Royal Academy, to which he was elected an Associate Member (ARA) in 1944. But he is 'popular' in the best and widest sense of the term. His appeal as a painter covers a catholic spectrum of taste. He is acceptable as much to the pundits of the quality journals as to less exalted scribblers. If the one appreciates the frequently double-edged subtlety of his subject matter and the brilliance of his technical expertise, the other can find at least an area of understanding in paintings such as *The Kiss*. The one may see it as a snide comment, the other may concentrate on a sniffle of romance. Such paintings often provide a talking point at the Academy's annual Summer Exhibitions. Ruskin Spear's passage to election was not a smooth one. His name was proposed by A. R. Middleton Todd in 1942. In 1944, the year of Sir Alfred Munnings' election to the Presidency of the Royal Academy, Ruskin Spear was officially invited to accept Associate Membership. He did so, and was duly elected. Afterwards, as he recalled to me, he was told that Munnings had done everything he could to persuade other members not to vote for him. I asked him if he knew why this was so since, being the generous-minded man that he is, Ruskin Spear has often spoken well to me of Sir Alfred. 'Well, you know,' he replied, 'Munnings was a great society man – anybody on a horse was fine! But I think the idea of a working-class cockney joining the establishment was a bit much for him! I imagine my subject matter was also a bit suspect [40]. Still, we became quite good friends over the years, although he always considered me potentially *dangerous*; always likely to propose one of those "modern chaps" for election. As you know,

40 *Mother and Child*
(1944)
Oil on essex board
36 x 24 in (91 x 61 cm)
Private collection

This tender study of a
mother potting her baby
was one of the artist's
submissions for the
Royal Academy
Summer Exhibition of
1947. However, it
provoked the extreme
displeasure of the
President, Sir Alfred
Munnings, and the artist
was obliged to remove it
before the exhibition
opened.

41 *Portrait of Rodney Burn*
(1962)
Oil on canvas
31 x 24 in (79 x 61 cm)
Exhibited Royal Academy
Summer Exhibition, 1962;
Royal Academy
Retrospective Exhibition,
1980
Collection: the artist (on
permanent loan to the
Royal College of Art)

Rodney Burn was a
teaching colleague at the
Royal College of Art. The
conception is notable for its
warm informality. Nothing
is posed or arranged. The
delicate nuances of colour,
based on a theme of green
and lilac, are sharpened into
vitality by the bold red of the
cigarette packet.

42 *Alastair Paterson QC*
(1960)
Oil on canvas
30 x 40 in (76 x 102 cm)
Collection: Alastair
Paterson QC, Toronto

Munnings was a ferocious anti-modernist. You wouldn't dare mention Picasso to him!'

During the forty years that have passed since Ruskin Spear's election – he was made a full Member (RA) in 1954 – the Royal Academy has moved forward under a succession of enlightened and imaginative Presidents to acquire and enjoy international recognition and prestige, not only for the many great exhibitions it has mounted but for the fact that, through the influence of adventurous and broad-minded Members like Ruskin Spear, many distinguished painters and sculptors who would not at one time have been offered Membership – or, even if they had, would have refused it – are now happy to belong to the Academy. In recent years Balthus, Miro, Chagall and Manzu have all accepted Honorary Membership. Ruskin Spear sees the election of William Roberts in 1958 as perhaps his most important success in introducing an artist of the avant garde into the Academy.

To understand the work of an artist it is necessary to understand the whole man. His work and his personality are closely interwoven. The breadth and vision of Ruskin Spear's art is reflected in his long, warm, and fruitful relationship with the Royal Academy, which has been his main shopwindow, but his highly controversial and

52

43 *Lord Butler of Saffron Walden* (1975)
Oil on canvas
40 x 30 in (102 x 76 cm)
Exhibited Royal Academy
Summer Exhibition, 1980
Collection: University of Essex

stimulatingly provocative disposition has been most clearly expressed in his years as one of England's most influential teachers. Between the years 1941 and 1950 he taught at Croydon, St Martin's, the Central and Hammersmith schools of art. But it was at the Royal College of Art that he made his mark as an outstanding and revolutionary teacher. He became a tutor in the Painting School of the Royal College in 1948, joining Carel Weight who was Professor of Paint-

ing. These two remarkable men – both highly distinctive artists – fostered the generation of Peter Blake, Frank Auerbach, David Hockney, Ron Kitaj and Allen Jones, all in their way intensely individual painters. It is unlikely that the system of art teaching which operated in Britain before the 1960s could have actively participated in the fostering of such rare talents. 'Classical' art school education was based on a strict and inflexible system. The method was

44 *Lord Adrian* (*c.* 1952–3)
Oil on canvas
30 x 25 in (76 x 63 cm)
Collection: Trinity College,
Cambridge

There is another version of
this portrait in the
Cavendish Laboratory,
Cambridge.

divided into a series of hallowed areas. The student began his education in the Antique room. After a while, and when his teachers thought he had gained sufficient expertise in the pencilled representation of such sacred cows as the *Venus de Milo, The Discobolus, The Belvedere Torso* and *The Boy with a Thorn*, he would be allowed into the life class. Painting from life and from still-life followed. The whole system was supported by the clinical attention of a teacher who demonstrated where the unfortunate student had gone wrong. 'Let me sit down' was invariably the opening gambit to this process of correction. The teacher would then proceed to make neat little drawings on the student's paper, purporting to demonstrate why his fore-shortening of the right leg had failed, in what way the anatomical construction of the left knee was wrong. (Anatomy was taught as a separate subject.) It was an entirely mechanistic system, dispassionate and

54

totally unrelated to the individual. It offered no opportunities for creative thought.

But in the late 1950s and early 1960s the system was overturned. Students entering the Royal College at this time, in many cases themselves the victims of this method of teaching, were suddenly awakened from their comfortable academic slumber by tutors like Ruskin Spear. The long, dead sleep and the mechanistic system were instantly dissolved and they were faced with entirely new concepts. Under Sir Robin Darwin, tutors at the Royal College were given a completely free hand to work as they liked with their students. *There were no rules.* Tutors were not even called upon to teach at any time except when they *felt* like teaching. 'In consequence,' Ruskin Spear told me, 'we did a lot of teaching. The atmosphere tingled with the excitement of being *free.*' Spear's approach to the problems of teaching was highly imaginative. The main axis of his method was to provoke, to incite his students to *think.* Mechanical drawing and painting *per se* was discouraged. The objective was to overthrow all the existing concepts and ideas which had already clouded the minds of students arriving at the College from their provincial forcing houses. Armed to the teeth with technical facilities, these were at once thrown into doubt. 'If we discussed drawing', Spear said, 'I directed their attention not to Michelangelo but to Thurber. When we discussed the mechanics of seeing, I would sometimes refer to Munnings who lost an eye early in life and

48 *Nude* (c. 1938)
Pen and ink and red chalk
$12\frac{1}{4} \times 21\frac{1}{4}$ in (31 x 54 cm)
Private collection

47 *Figure on a Bed* (1944)
Oil on board
25 x 30 in (63 x 76 cm)
Collection: Usher Gallery,
Lincoln

who, I believe, painted all the better for that. A painter sees with one eye. If he sees with both eyes he becomes a sculptor. Immediately there would be cross-references to literature – to H. G. Wells' *Country of the Blind*, where the one-eyed man was King. I got them to *read*. And since they usually arrived at the College well satisfied with their ability to produce proficient drawings of the figure, I argued that painting should come first and that one should learn to draw by exploring and resolving some of the problems of painting. After all, painting *is* drawing, if not in the strictly linear sense. When you went into any of the rooms where students were working, you went in to cross swords with them.'

The basis of these attacking arguments

was the intention to liberate the student from the shackles of set criteria, and at the same time to precipitate him into a vacuum in which he would be compelled to re-think – to re-evaluate – his whole philosophy of art, practical and theoretical. Students of real ability very soon found new directions, and discovered who and what they were and where their affiliations lay. For the artist, the primary problem is one of *identity*. Bad teaching imposes a false identity upon the student, the identity of the teacher.

Ruskin Spear is entertaining about such life drawing as was taught at the College, and the light it throws upon the personality both of the teacher and the taught. 'In Johnny Minton's room', he said, 'the students worked only from male models. In

mine they drew only from female models. All the "intellectuals" flocked to Johnny!' Teaching is not all plain sailing. Conflict among the tutors can lead to some startling results. There is a delightful nuance of self-deprecation in one story Ruskin Spear has to tell. One of his students – now a successful portrait painter – was taken to task for what Spear considered to be a wrongly toned background. Having repainted it himself, Spear remarked 'That's the tone!' and he left the room. Almost immediately Robert Buhler walked in and said to the same student: 'That's the wrong tone', and promptly repainted it quite differently. At that point in his career the student was a rather colourful painter. However, the trauma of these conflicting views was so great that he immediately moved into a monochromatic scale, and has since worked more or less exclusively in black, grey and white.

Ruskin Spear was perfectly in accord with the mood of the early Sixties: partly iconoclastic, partly seeking the security of new directions. The sound of the Beatles and the scent of flower power filled the air. Pop art, with the underfelt of a brash but exciting junk culture, had already burst upon the American scene.

Roy Lichenstein and Robert Rauschenberg, with their witty allusions to the strip cartoon, and their adaptations of popular imagery from commercial art themes (Rauschenberg was the first Pop artist to combine actual objects, such as coca cola

50 *Chicken Madras* (1984)
Oil on board
16 x 12 in (41 x 30 cm)
Private collection

49 *Sid James* (1962)
Oil on canvas
48 x 36 in (122 x 91 cm)
Exhibited Royal Academy
Retrospective Exhibition,
1980
Private collection

A painting which should be
considered primarily on its
abstract and asymmetrical
qualities.

bottles with the other elements of his picture making) offered a stimulating fresh direction that was eagerly and fruitfully exploited by such young men as Hockney, Kitaj and Allen Jones. All three artists were students of Spear and Weight, and there is little doubt that the climate of freedom they enjoyed at the College must have been a crucial factor in the evolution of their art at this time.

In a much less conspicuous way, Ruskin Spear is himself, by implication, a 'popular'

painter. His pictures frequently contain cross-references to the imagery of advertising as it appears on street hoardings and in public houses (**30, 51**). He was therefore already sympathetic to the emergence of fully-fledged Pop art when it arrived. His art is an intrinsic part of the iconography of contemporary popular art.

It is not surprising that in 1957 Ruskin Spear was invited to show a selection of his pictures in a mixed exhibition of British painting presented in the Pushkin Museum, Moscow. In 1956, together with Carel Weight, Paul Hogarth, Derek Greaves and others, he had taken part in an exhibition called 'Looking at People' at the South London Art Gallery, Camberwell. The exhibition attracted the attention of representatives from the Union of Soviet Artists and, at their invitation, the exhibition was promptly transferred to Moscow. The strong social realist flavour of the pictures must have seemed the epitome of British proletarianism. Here was the working man in his natural environment, complete with his pubs, cafés and cloth caps. How the

51 *The Old Lyric Theatre,*
Hammersmith, 1943 (1979)
Oil on board
31 x 39 in (79 x 99 cm)
Exhibited Royal Academy
Summer Exhibition, 1979;
Royal Academy
Retrospective Exhibition,
1980
Private collection

52 *The Woman next Door*
(*c.* 1961–2)
Oil on board
48 x 36 in (122 x 91 cm)
Exhibited Royal Academy
Summer Exhibition, 1966
Collection: the artist

Russians came to terms with *Haute Couture* is another matter.

The exhibition was packed with visitors every day of the three weeks it was on. Whenever the crowd thinned out it was promptly brought up to strength by 'persuading' passers-by from the street that they would enjoy the show, so the painter told me. He was with the exhibition for the whole time it was at the Pushkin, and became known as 'the people's artist'; not a *popular* artist, but a *people's* artist. The distinction, in terms of the venue, is en-

lightening.

A knowledge of the artist's working methods and the materials he elects to use are essential to a complete understanding of his work. Accident may play its part – Turner could not always have known how his water-colour would run, nor Jackson Pollock exactly how his paint would drip. But such fortuitous instances apart, art is the product of a highly complex interplay of cerebral and physical factors. What colours does the painter use? On what surface does he prefer to paint? What medium – if any –

54 *Fred's Day by the Sea*
(1975)
Oil on canvas
48 x 36 in (122 x 91 cm)
Exhibited Royal Academy
Summer Exhibition, 1975;
Royal Academy
Retrospective Exhibition,
1980
Private collection

The Englishman's day out needs to be uncomfortable: cap, tie and suit, and the pebbles of a south coast resort all help to make the occasion disagreeable. Later there will be endless queues for tea and snacks. Fred hardly exists against the splendour of the massive sea wall, which the painter has built up with heavy encrustations of paint.

53 *Sherry Bar Portrait*
(1964)
Oil on canvas
38½ x 26½ in (98 x 67 cm)
Exhibited Royal Academy
Summer Exhibition, 1964
Private collection

This was painted in the Ravenscourt Arms, Hammersmith, which — according to the artist — was where Dylan Thomas did his early morning 'light drinking' in the late 1940s. (Since at that time the pub had no toilet facilities, it had no spirits licence.) Ruskin and Dylan often met here for a sober drink.

does he employ to mix his colours? Ruskin Spear has elaborated on all these points, and as I discuss them it will become evident how closely the intellectual, emotive and physical elements are interwoven in his work. The orchestration of the artist's colour is based on the following palette: windsor blue (at one time generally known as monastral blue), ultramarine, yellow ochre, raw umber, cadmium and lemon yellow, cadmium red, Indian red, light red, alizarin crimson, permanent green (deep), viridian, ivory black and flake white. His chromatic scale varies widely, from brilliant, highly-pitched schemes to more subfusc low-pitched harmonies. The colour plates should be studied both in relation to Spear's total range of colours and to the modifications and restrictions the demands of a particular subject might impose upon him. He can draw upon an extensive colour keyboard, which he always uses with

55 *Arnold Goodman*
(*c.* 1960)
Oil on canvas
30 x 25 in (76 x 63 cm)
Collection: Beaverbrook
Art Gallery, Fredericton,
New Brunswick, Canada

subtlety and discretion. If a note of discord is called for, he has the means to express it. His orchestrations can range from the strident rawness of the portrait of Barnett Newman to the exquisitely delicate colour and tonal gradations of *Poet Laureate Afloat*. In each instance the approach is exactly right.

The surface on which he most likes to paint is hardboard. Sometimes he works on paper and, for commissioned portraits, on canvas. 'Because', as he says, 'a paying sitter doesn't feel he is getting his money's worth *unless* he is portrayed on canvas! It's just a silly, traditional idea.' Toned surfaces suit him best. 'If you work on a coloured surface', he says, 'it starts you off on some-

thing you would never have thought of if you had begun to paint on a white background. I often work on a surface to which I have given a coat of viridian and white, applied quite thickly, and mixed with turps so that it dries matt. Or perhaps I might work on a coat of light red and white. The effect of putting a contrasting or brilliant colour on to such a coloured surface is quite different from putting it straight on a white background. So from the word go you have a stimulus, an excitement that can push you into provoking chromatic schemes as you begin to build up your colours and work out the subject.' In this way, the effect is intensified and redirected by the evolution of

56 *The White Hat* (1972)
Oil on canvas
28 x 36 in (71 x 91 cm)
Exhibited Royal Academy
Summer Exhibition, 1972;
Royal Academy
Retrospective Exhibition,
1980
Collection: Derek
Winterbottom

colour orchestrations that add a depth, warmth, atmosphere or sensation, all of which develop, often unexpectedly, as the painter works.

Ruskin Spear's paintings often possess this quality of a continuous coming into being. There is an inconclusiveness in the 'final' result: it is never literally final but grows, not only in terms of the artist's unending pursuit of the revelation that the work of art acquires as it unfolds, but also in relation to the responses which the spectator brings to bear upon it. The totality of an artist's conception is never completely released because it is always developing. The mystery of what he wishes, or tries, to say can never be resolved.

Supreme examples of this continuous 'coming into being' – of the image only partially released – are to be found in the carvings of Rodin. Faces, hands, bodies emerge and break the surface of the marble, moving into the light from the heart of the stone. Ecstasy locks the closed eyelids, long fingers lie intertwined, hair runs in rivers, but still the marble holds the mystery of what is unrevealed. This is the true nature of art. Technique is not the means to an end; it is simply the prelude to a beginning. What is unsaid is what matters. The sudden revelation of unforeseen colour relationships evolving as the artist works endows Ruskin

57 *Girl with Black Hair*
(1948)
Oil on canvas
30 x 20 in (76 x 51 cm)
Collection: the artist

Spear's art with an ambiguity without which art becomes static and totally revealed – not in depth, but in the shallowness of pseudo-art, such as in so many commissioned portraits, or in those areas of commercial and graphic design which demand 'completeness'.

The true artist is a seeker. Again I quote Picasso[6]: 'When I paint, my object is to show what I have found and not what I am looking for. . .' Rodin finds the image in the marble, Ruskin Spear the colour in the eye of a cat. But there is always something more to be found, and in this process the spectator has a vital role to play. The artist must leave room for this factor to operate, since the interpretation of the subject is as much the province of the spectator as it is his; perhaps more so since the painter, like the sculptor, can never be certain either what he will discover or what remains to be discovered.

There are many areas of beauty in a work

58 *Ida* (*c.* 1936)
Oil on canvas
50 x 40 in (127 x 101 cm)
Collection: Don Steyn,
Fosse Gallery,
Stowe-on-the-Wold,
Gloucestershire

of art, not only in the subject itself but also in the technical means by which the painter or sculptor executes its creation: the marks of the sculptor's chisel; the energy that he transmits to the clay as he works it with his fingers; the *matière* and the impasto of the painter's brushwork. Ruskin Spear is not in favour of the palette knife as an instrument with which to paint. 'The knife is only a tool for mixing colours', he explains. 'As an alternative to the brush it merely "irons out", flattens, destroys the vitality of the pigment, crushes its body. Paint should flow from the brush. It is a living, sensuous material. Brushwork is the flesh of a painting. Every hair of a brush contributes its own living mark, like the imprints of a sculptor's finger pressures in the clay.' The *matière* of a painting should have the animation of skin, with its infinite textural variations. Ruskin Spear combines a mixture of double mastic varnish, turpentine and linseed oil with his

59 *Oliver* (1984)
Oil on board
40 x 30 in (107 x 76 cm)
Exhibited Royal Academy
Summer Exhibition, 1984
Collection: Myrna Bustani

oil paint. Thick and rich, it is the perfect medium for an artist whose paint quality is dense and sensuous.

It is usually considered that an oil painting should be framed unglazed. Ruskin Spear prefers his oils to be glazed, for two reasons: in the first place, glass helps to protect the painting against the ravages of atmospheric pollution; but perhaps more importantly the reflections which it picks up, and which change continuously, add fresh dimensions of visual experience and sensation to the picture. Objects, people, faces, colour, light and shadow are all drawn into the painting through the glass, extending and altering its identity in endless ways. Glass, with its reflections, adds an ambiguity to the ex-

perience and sensation of looking. Excitement is intensified by the unexpected.

What an artist has to say about his work is not necessarily of importance. The Statements many artists write for books and exhibition catalogues usually fail because they are contrived for a special occasion. So often they are pretentious and obscurantist. Picasso's two Statements to Marius de Zayas and Christian Zervos, made respectively in 1923 and 1935, are the exception. In the second of these he virtually dismissed the need to talk about art: 'Everyone wants to understand art. Why not try to understand the songs of a bird? Why does one love the night, flowers, everything about one without trying to understand them? But in the

60 *Fiery Fred* (Fred Trueman, 1964)
Oil on board
82 x 26½ in (208 x 67 cm)
Exhibited Royal Academy
Summer Exhibition, 1964
Collection: The Lord's
Traverners (On loan to the
museum at Lord's Cricket
Ground)

case of a painting people have to understand. . .' Nevertheless, I did ask Ruskin Spear if there was anything he wished to add to this introductory note of mine, either about art in general or about his own art in particular. He had only one observation: 'I try to communicate. . .' His work speaks eloquently enough; he communicates much. Beyond this, the thoughts I have added about the nature of art, and about Ruskin Spear's work in relationship to these ideas may help to illuminate not only the significance of his *oeuvre* but also the complex processes by which it is created.

69

Notes

1 Jean Adhemar, *Graphic Art of the Eighteenth Century* (Thames and Hudson, London, 1984), p. 61.

2 Charles Merrill Mount, *John Singer Sargent: A Biography* (Cresset Press, 1957) p. 243

3 *The Hard-Won Image: Traditional Method and Subject in Recent British Art* (The Tate Gallery, 1984)

4 Conversations with Picasso: *Cahiers d'Art* (Paris, 1935) Vol. 10, No. 10, pp. 173–8

5 Ambroise Vollard, *Renoir: An Intimate Record* (New York, 1930) p. 118

6 Picasso's Statement to Marius de Zayas, published under the title *Picasso Speaks* (*The Arts*, New York, May 1923)

Acknowledgments

The author and publishers would like to thank the artist for the unsparing co-operation he has provided in the preparation of this book. They would also like to thank the following individuals, galleries and organizations for their help, and for permission to reproduce works in their collections: The Royal Academy of Arts; Professor Sir Lawrence Gowing CBE, ARA, who has acted as adviser and consultant; Kenneth J. Tanner MVO, Comptroller of The Royal Academy of Arts; Selina Fellows of The Royal Academy of Arts; Helen Valentine of The Royal Academy of Arts Library; Marie Levy who first read the text and made helpful suggestions; Sally Lunn who produced the author's two conversations with the artist for BBC Sound Archives (see p. 9); the Trustees of the Tate Gallery; the Governors of the Royal Shakespeare Theatre, Stratford; the Governors of the BBC; the Beaverbrook Art Gallery, Fredericton, New Brunswick, Canada; the Trustees of the Chantry Bequest; the Harris Museum and Art Gallery, Preston; Magdalene College, Cambridge; the Royal College of Art; the Crane Kalman Gallery, London; Trinity College, Cambridge; Don Steyn, Fosse Gallery, Stowe-on-the-Wold; De Beers Collection, London; Bill Michael OBE; Tony Stratton Smith; Jack Young; Mrs Desmond Heywood; Annette Halfin; David Whitehead; The Hon. Edwina Sandys; the Usher Gallery, Lincoln; Lady Gwendolen Herbert; Myrna Bustani; Derek Winterbottom; Anthony Brodie; Robert Buhler RA; Carel Weight RA; Alastair Paterson QC; Stuart McMillan; Philip Daubeny; The Lord's Taverners; The National Theatre, London; and, appropriately, the Victoria Inn and Christie's Tavern, Richmond, where the author often received flashes of inspiration.

61 *Cat and Flowers* (1983)
Oil on board
30 x 25 in (76 x 63 cm)
Private collection

Index

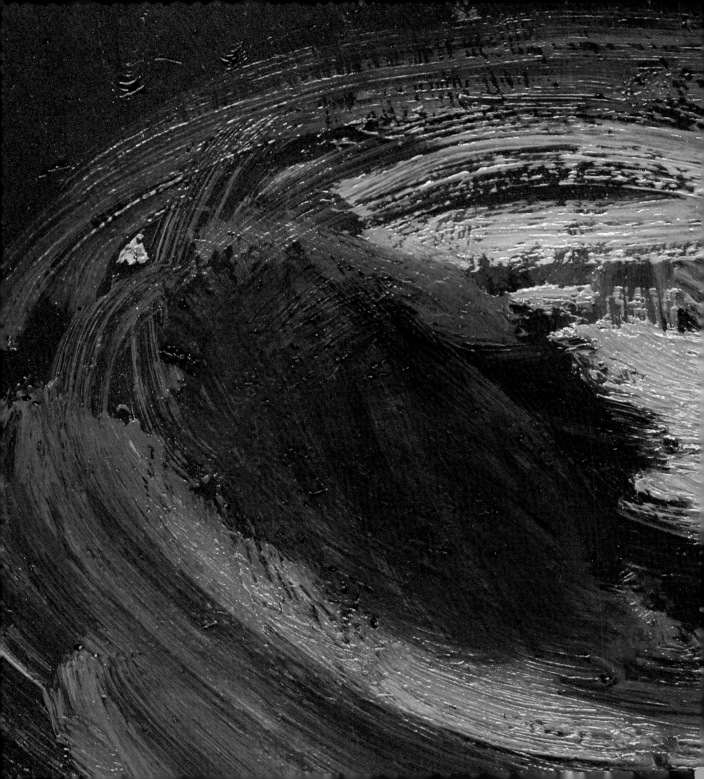